World Of Fantasy: How To Draw Mermaids And Magical Characters

Learn How to Draw Mermaids from Fantasy Stories

Mermaid Book

By : Gala Publication

2

Published By :

Gala Publication

© Copyright 2015 – Gala Publication

ISBN-13: **978-1522721529**
ISBN-10: **1522721525**

Table of Contents

BEAUTIFUL MERMAID

STEP 1

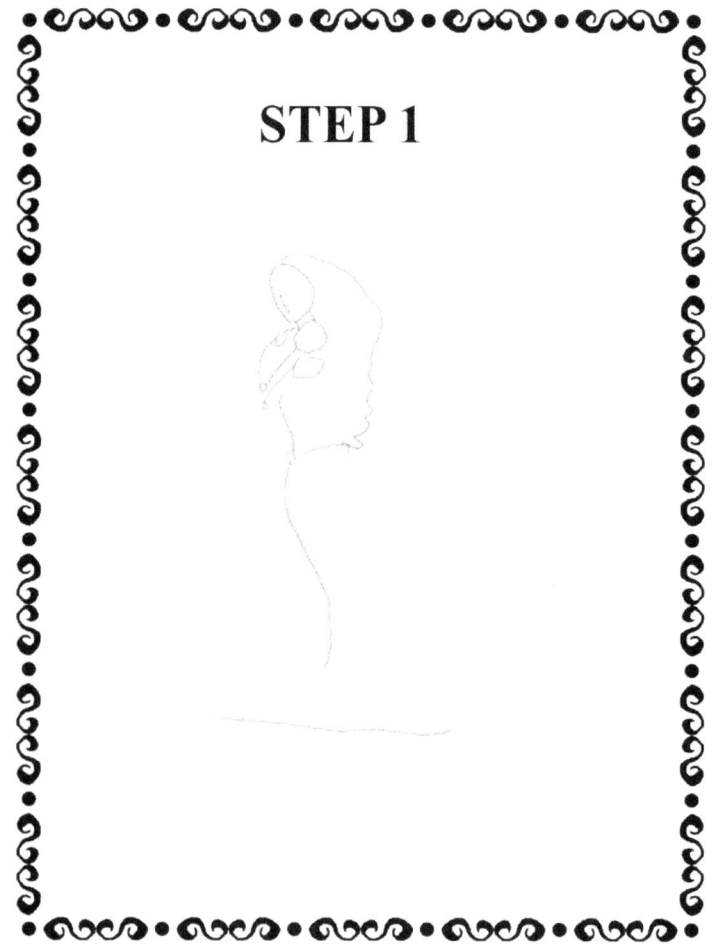

STEP 2

STEP 3

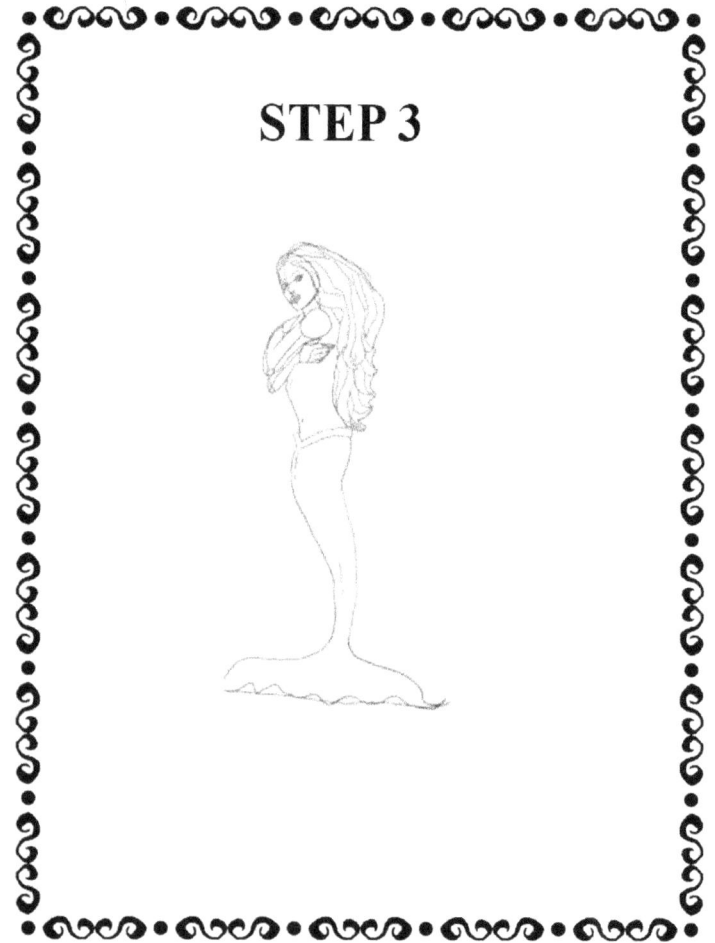

STEP 4

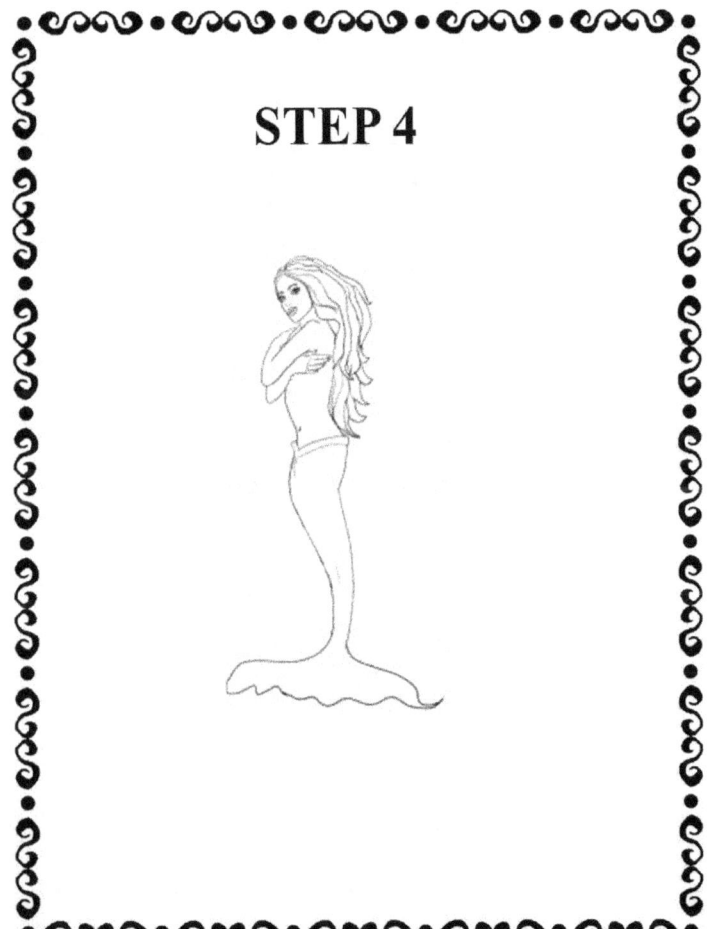

LITTLE MERMAID

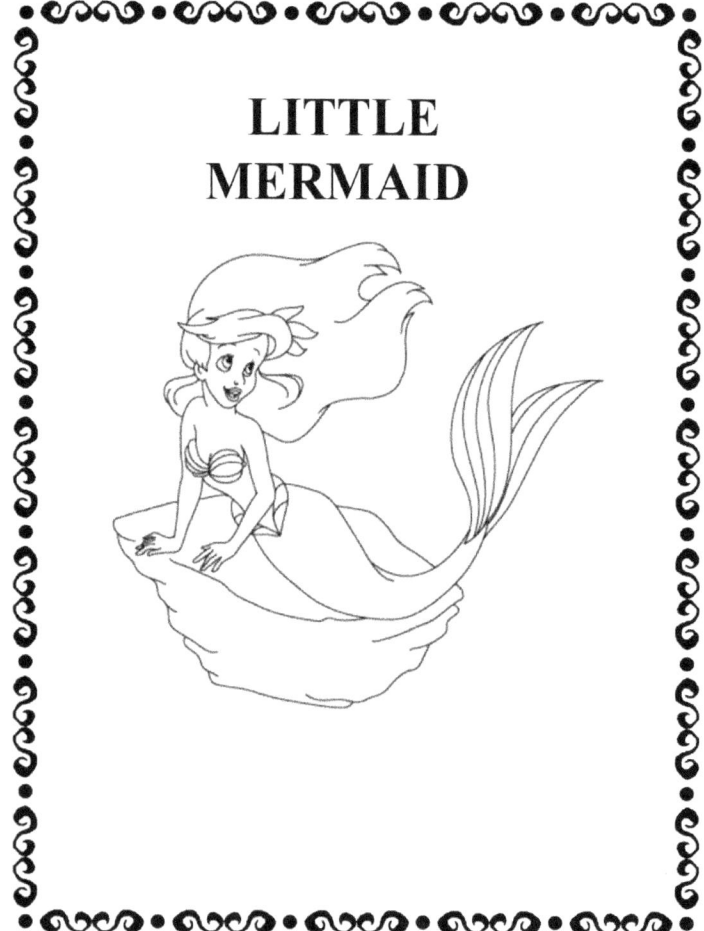

STEP 1

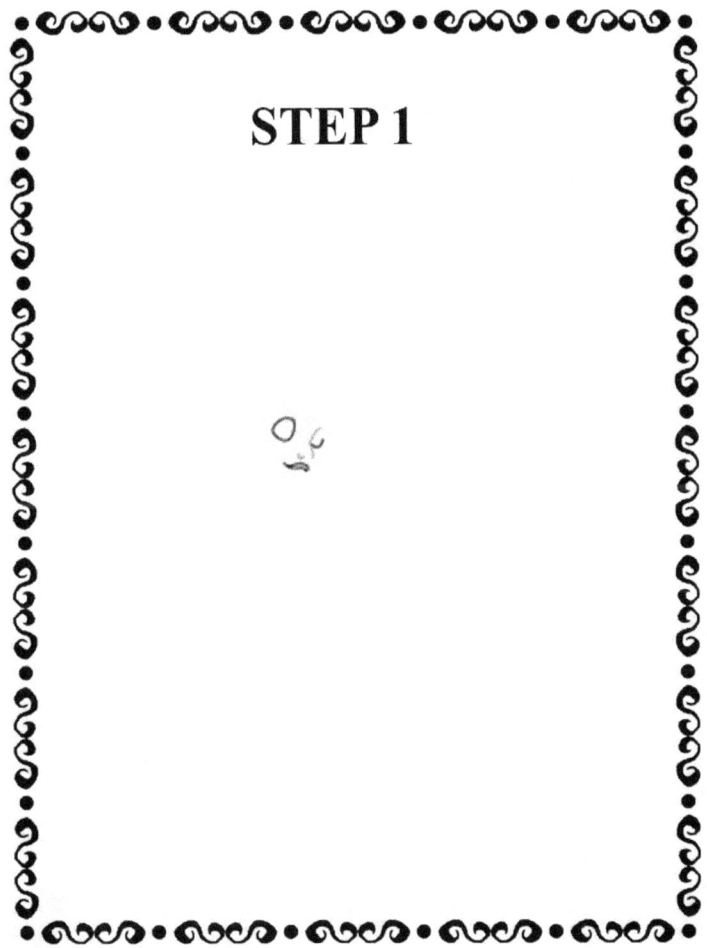

STEP 2

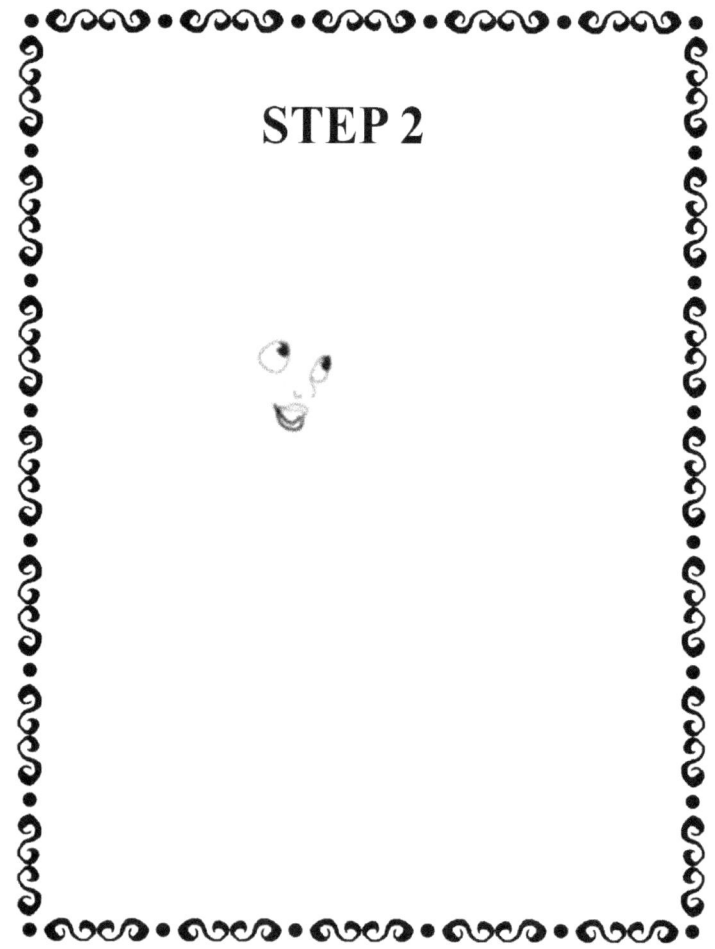

STEP 3

STEP 4

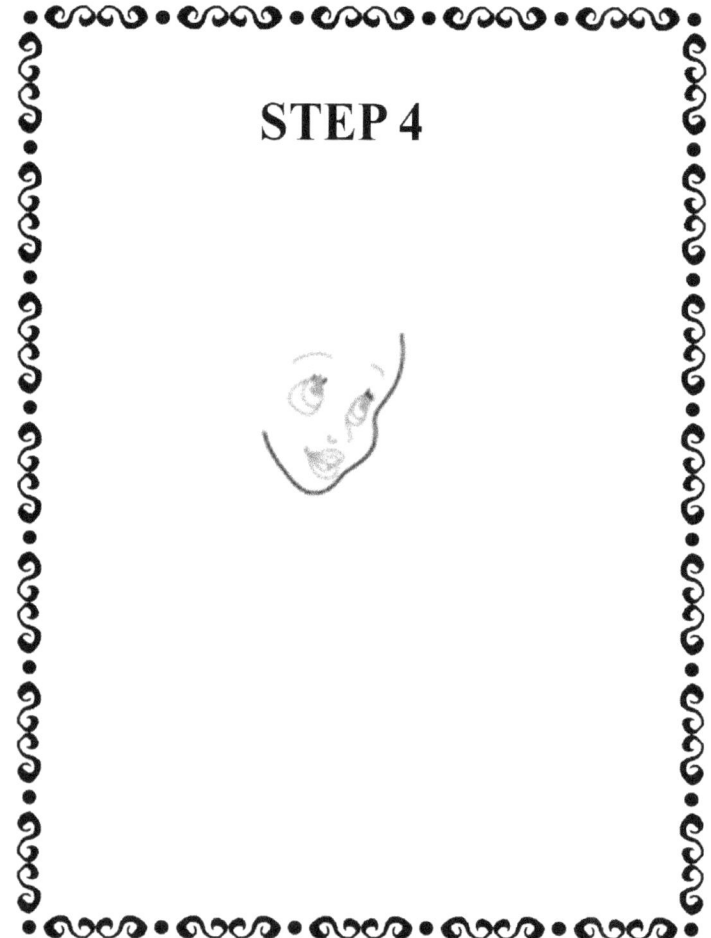

STEP 5

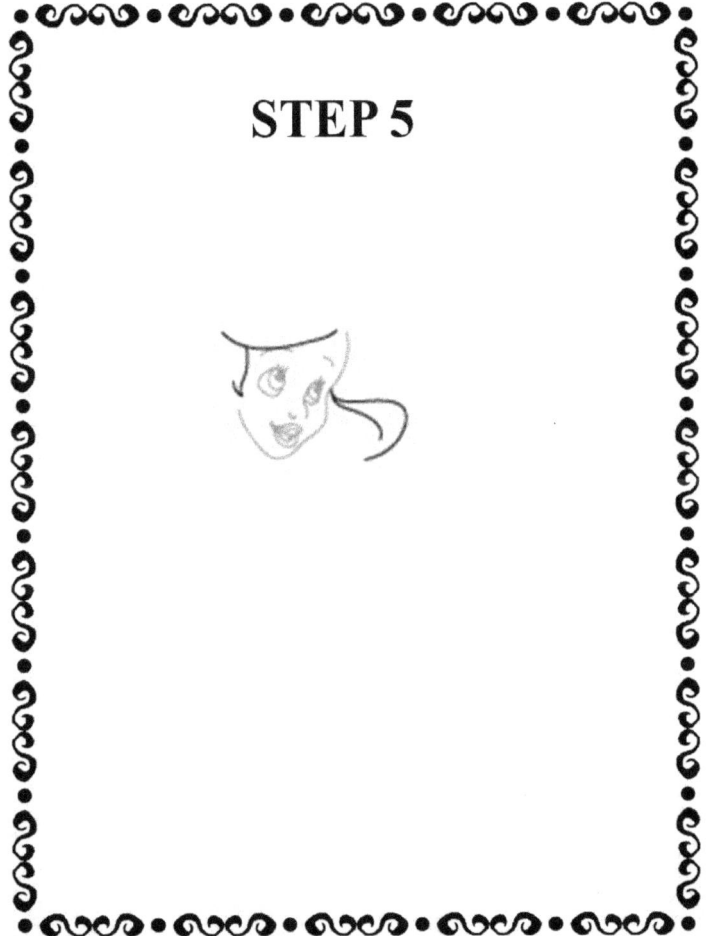

STEP 6

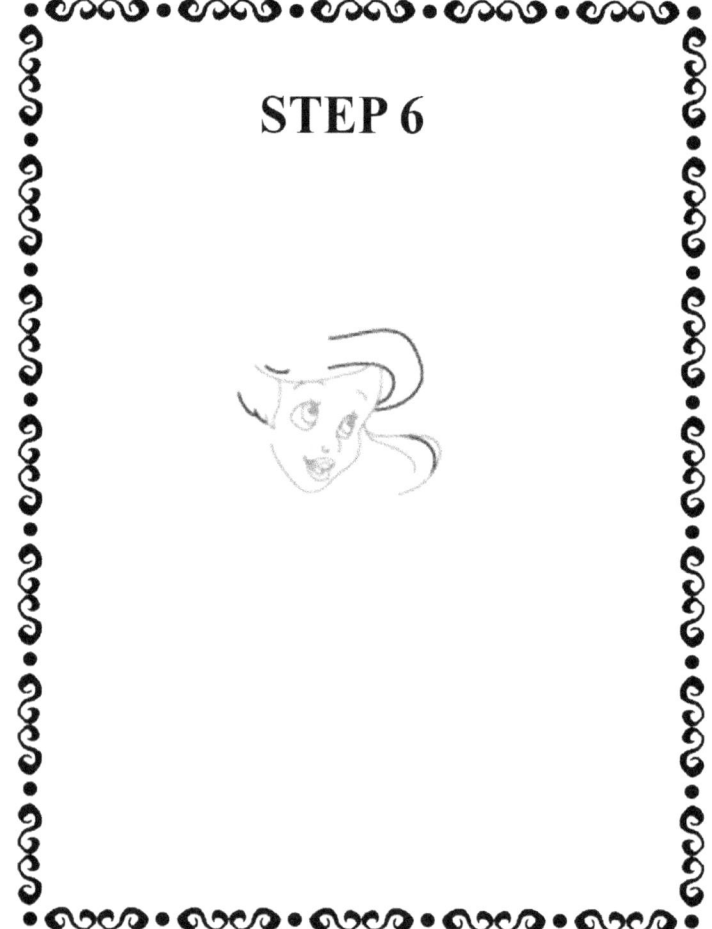

STEP 7

STEP 8

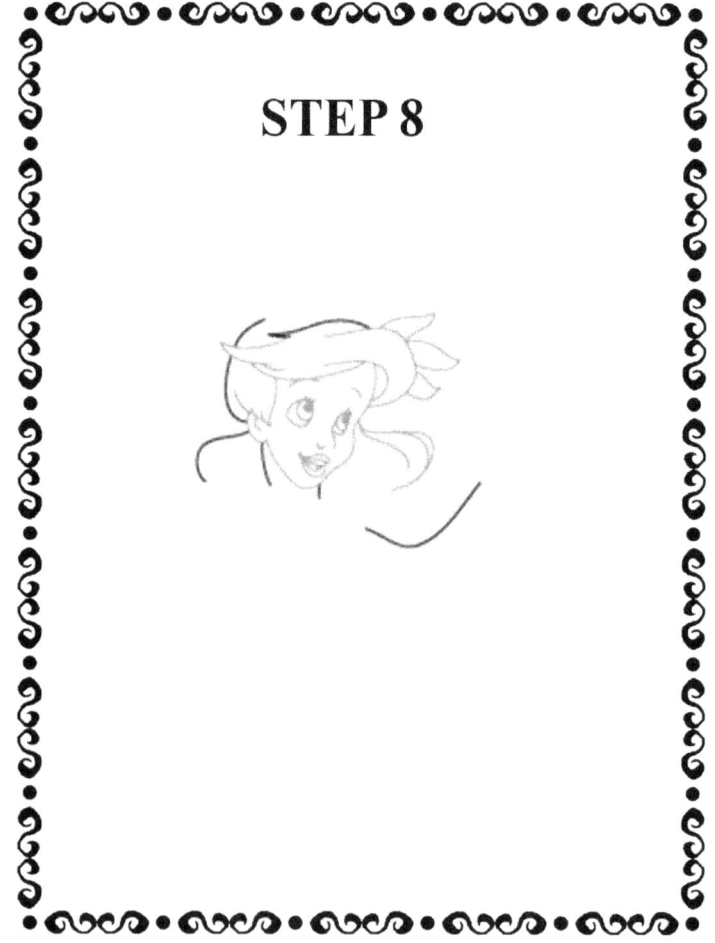

STEP 9

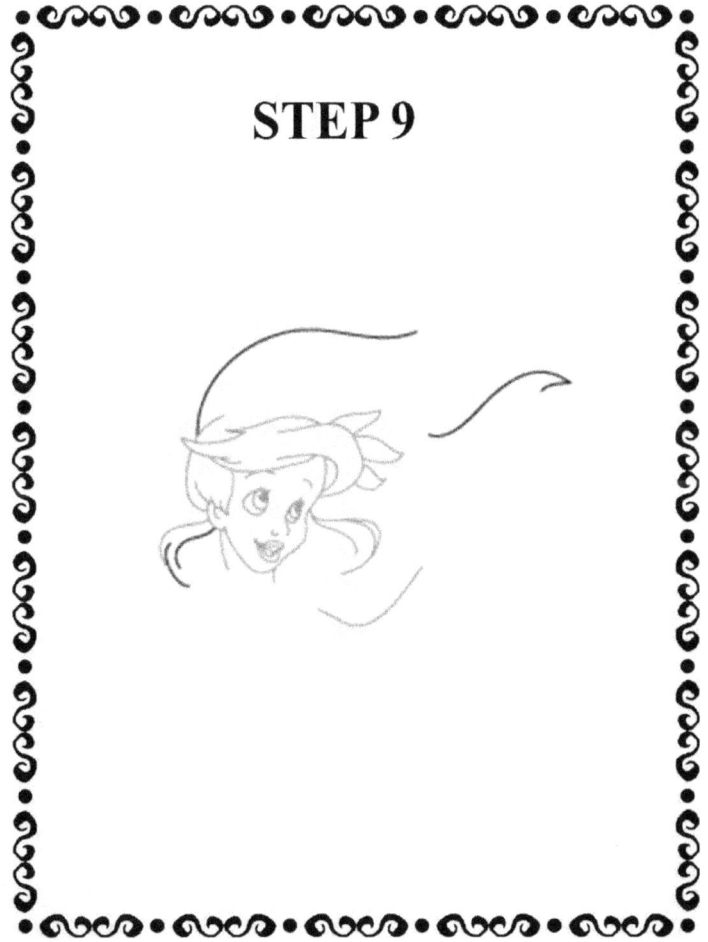

STEP 10

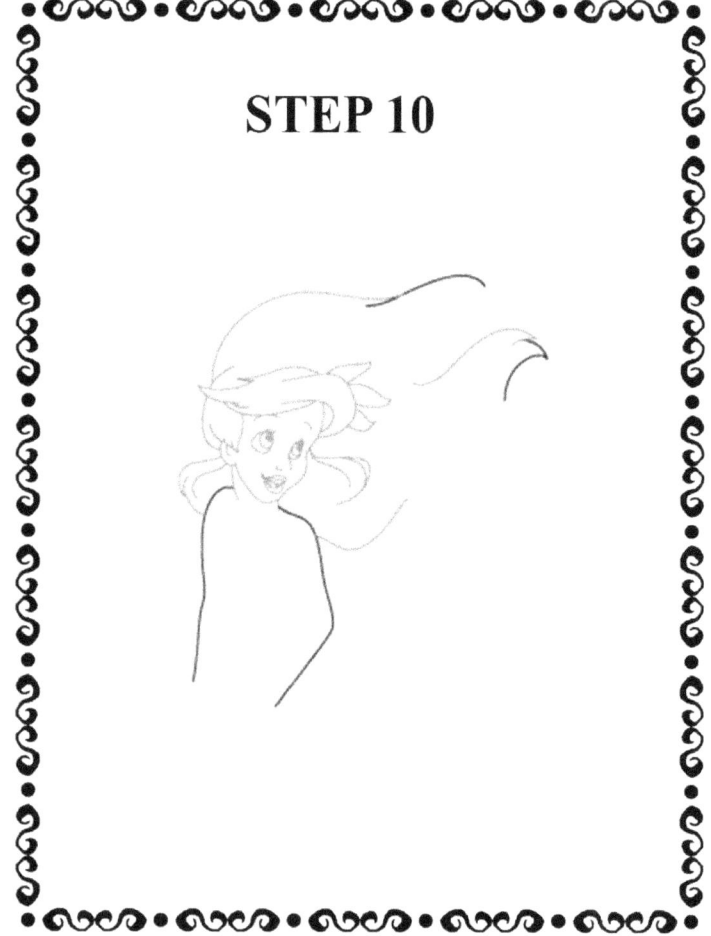

STEP 11

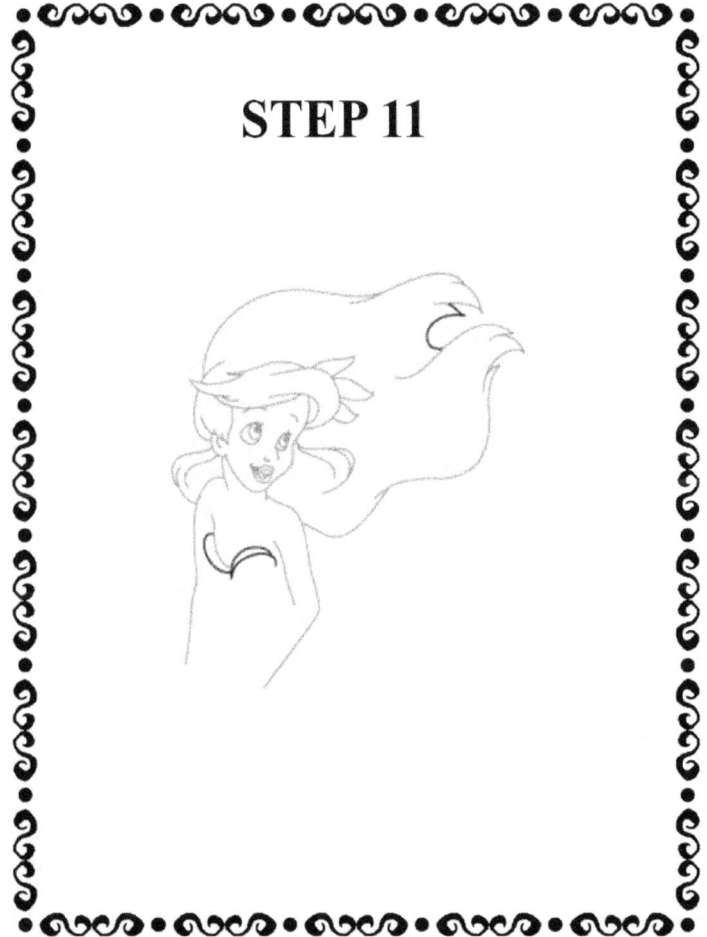

STEP 12

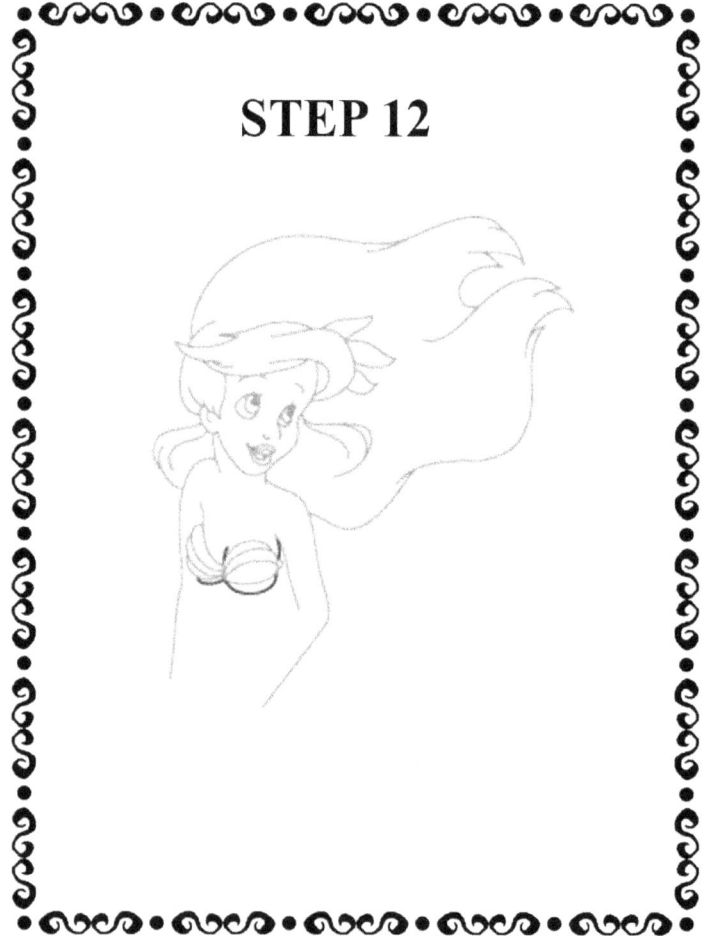

STEP 13

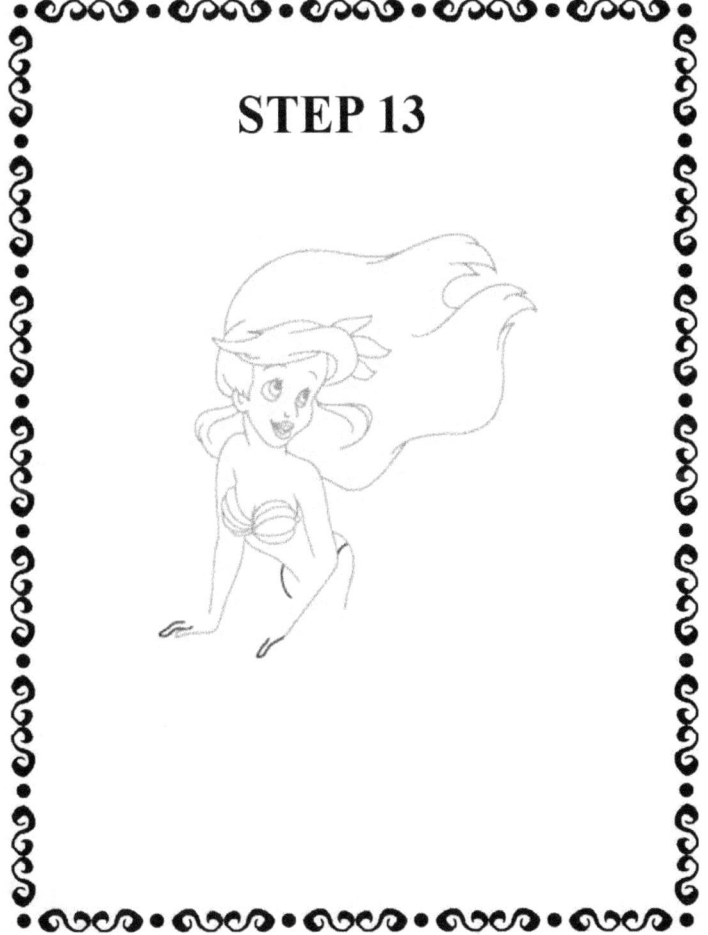

STEP 14

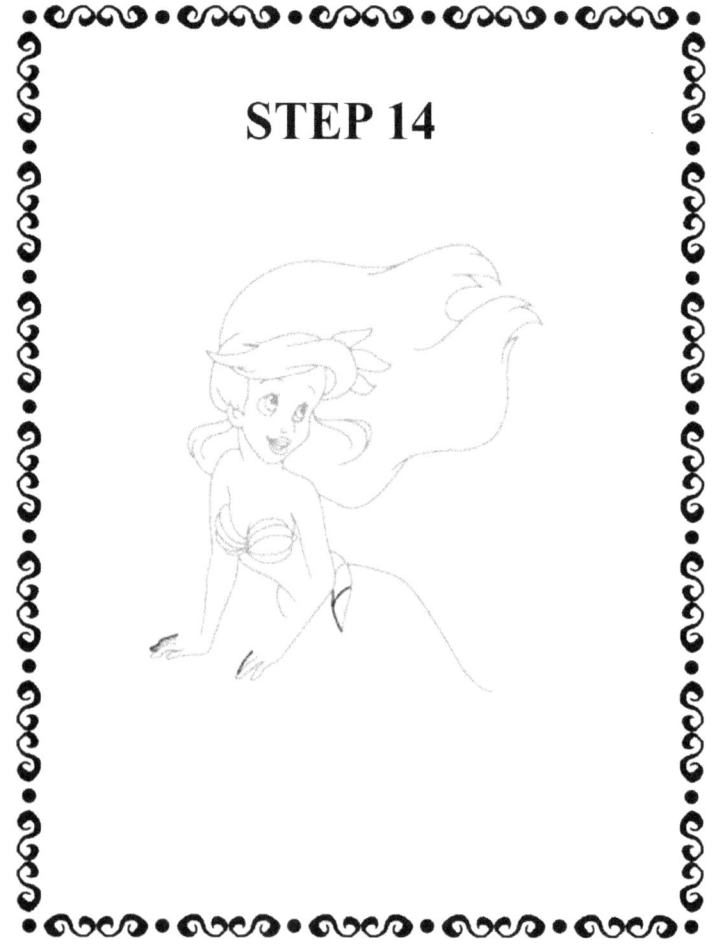

STEP 15

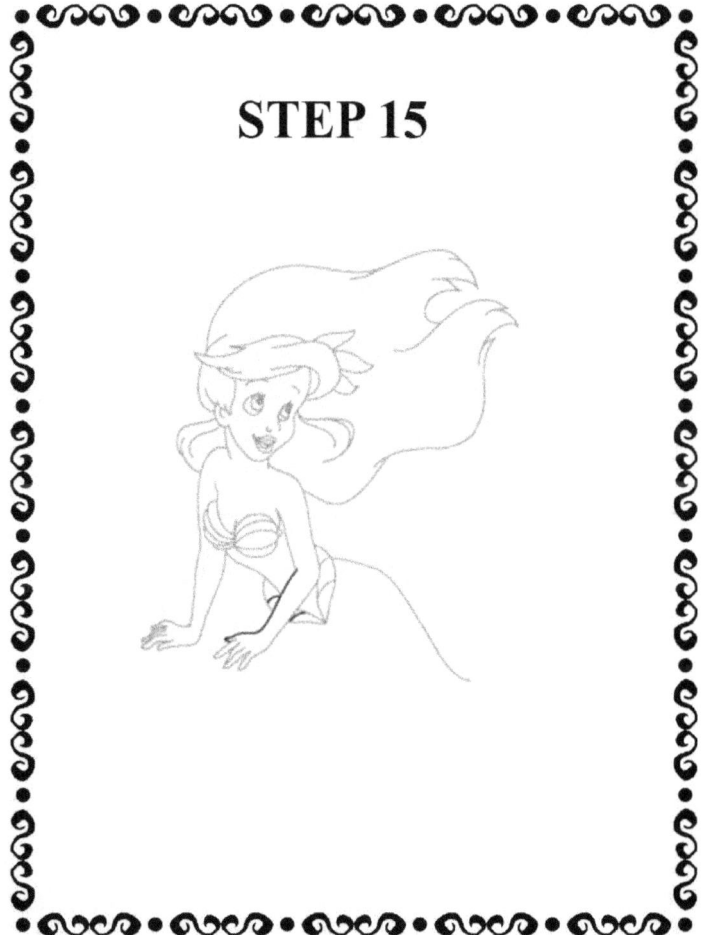

STEP 16

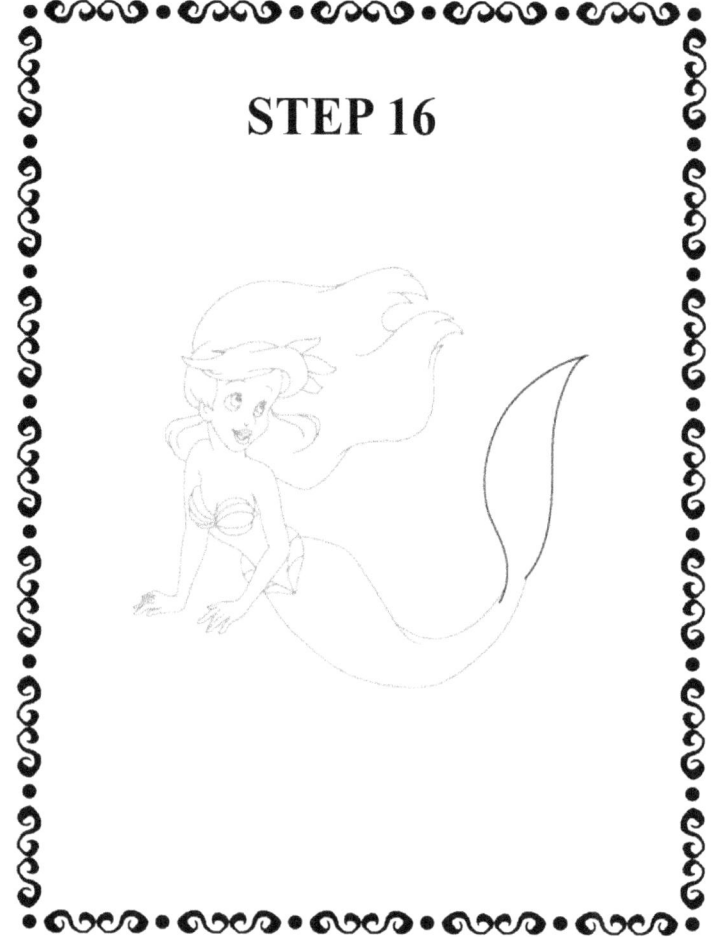

STEP 17

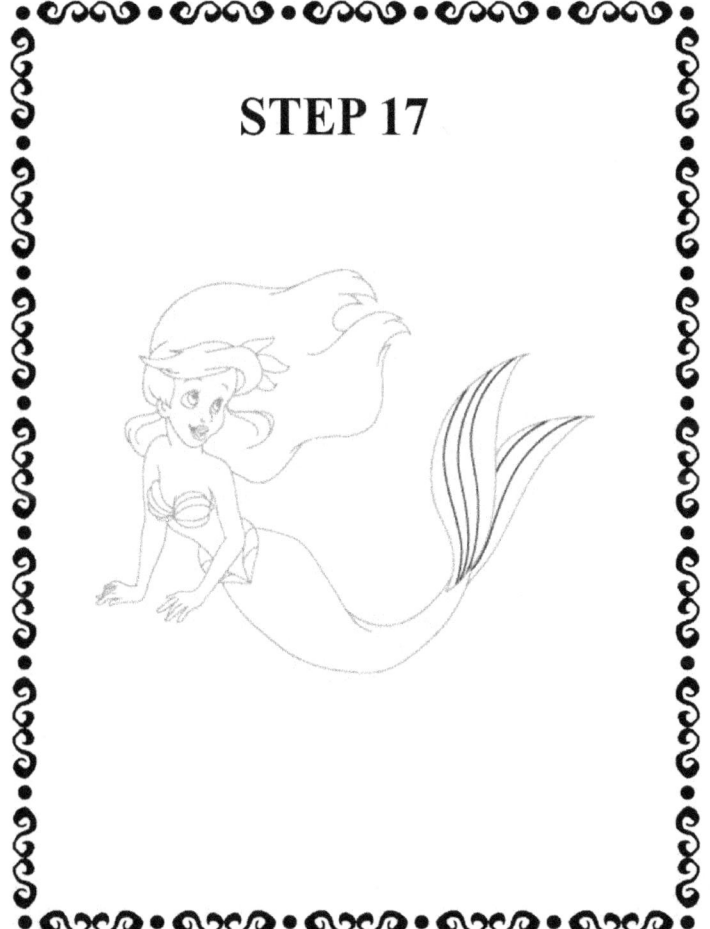

STEP 18

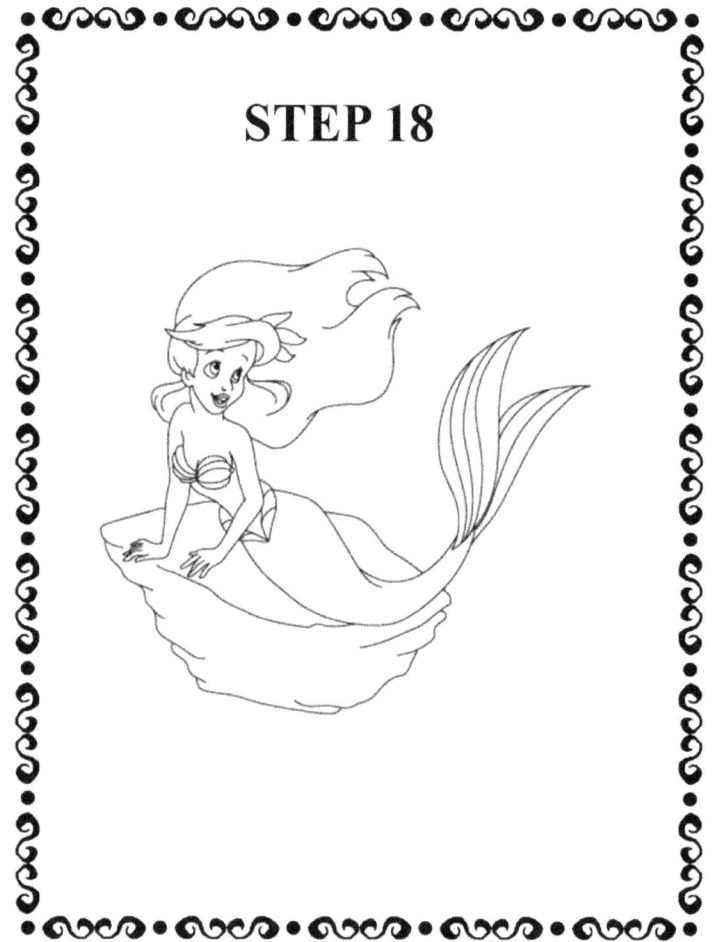

MERMAID FACE

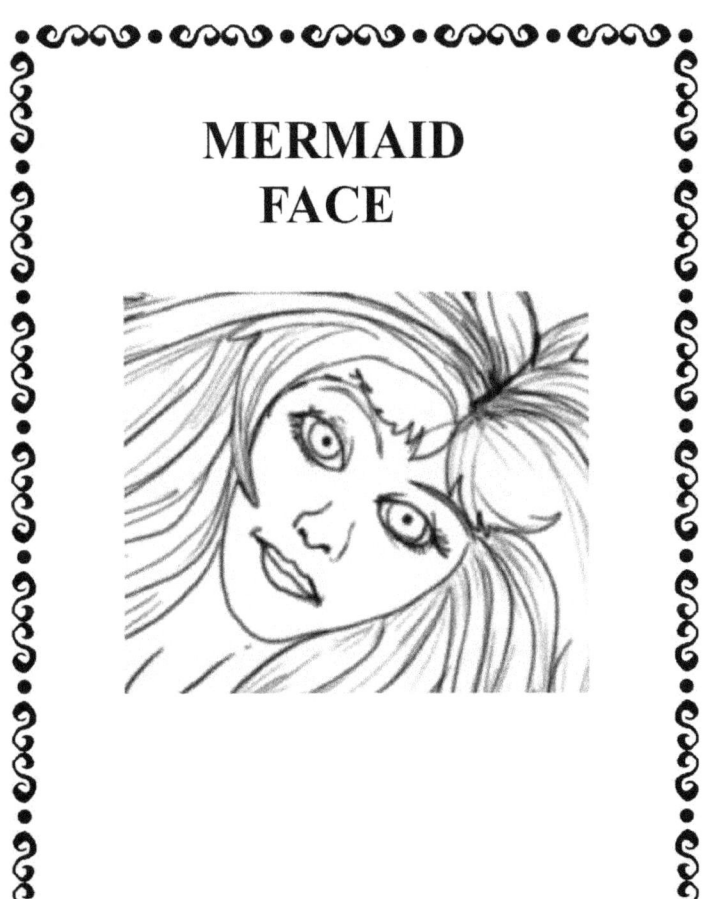

STEP 1

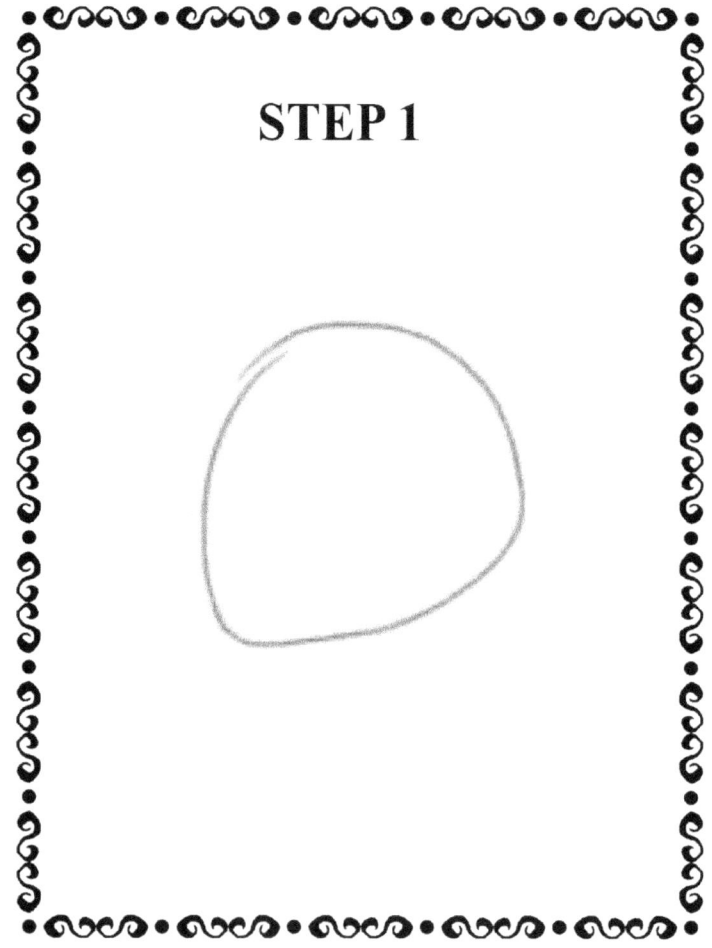

STEP 2

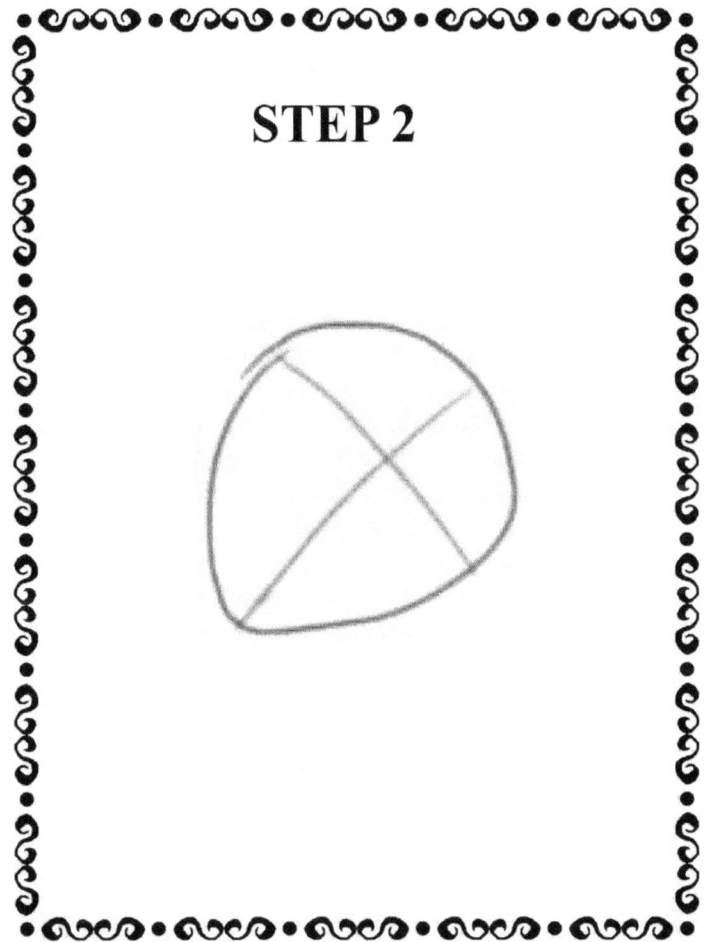

STEP 3

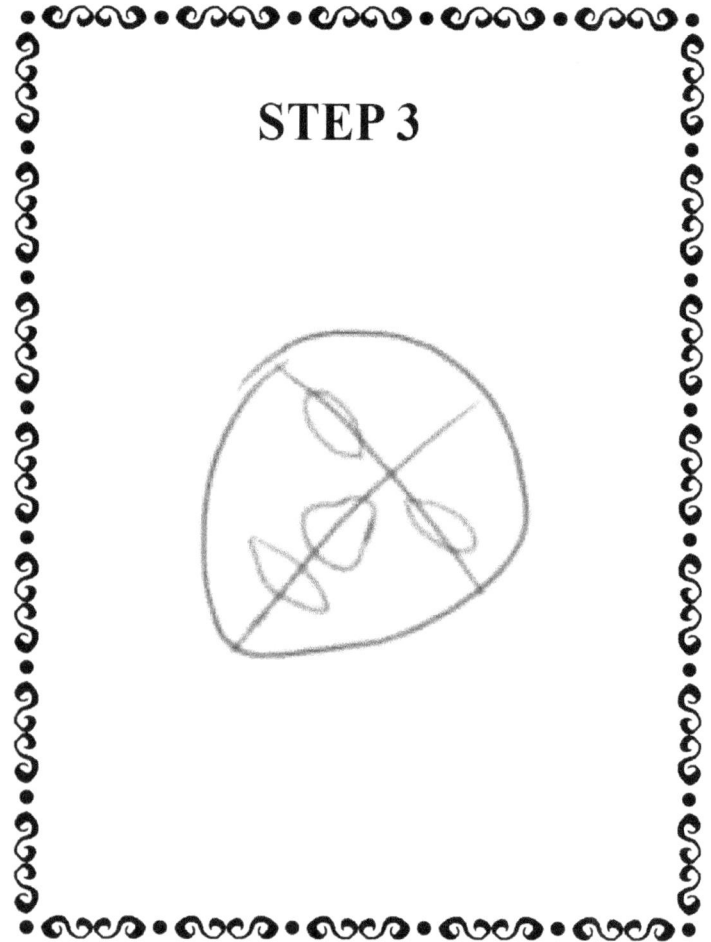

STEP 4

STEP 5

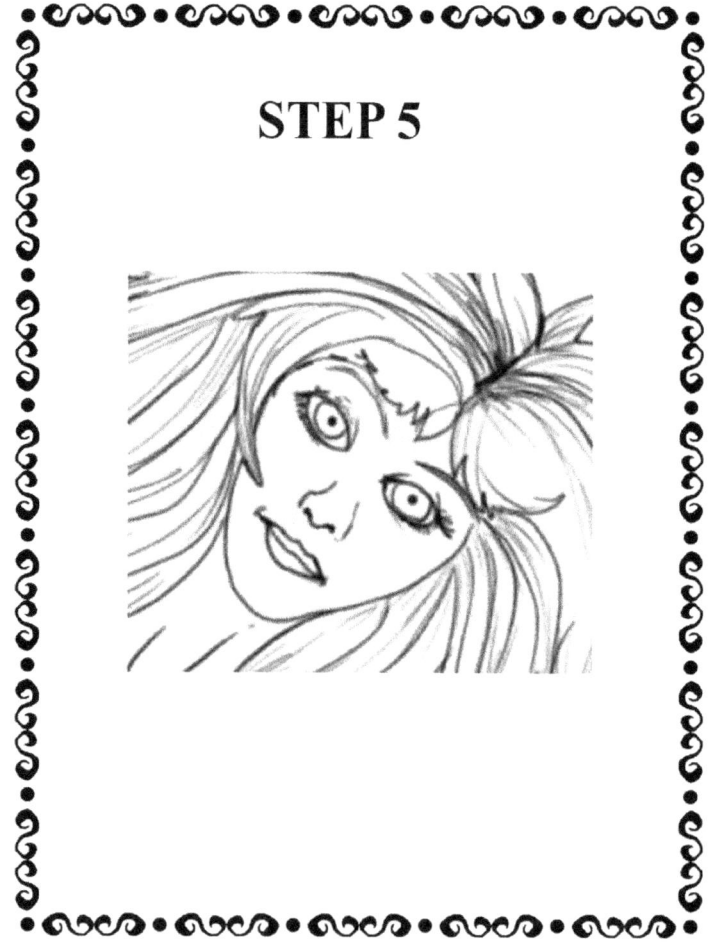

SEAWEED MERMAID

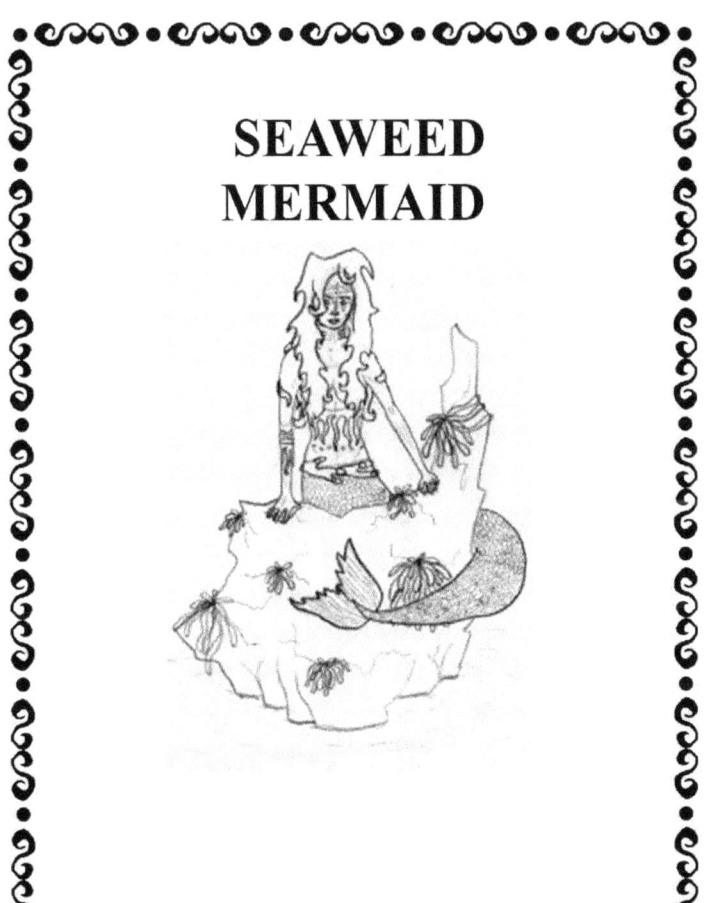

STEP 1

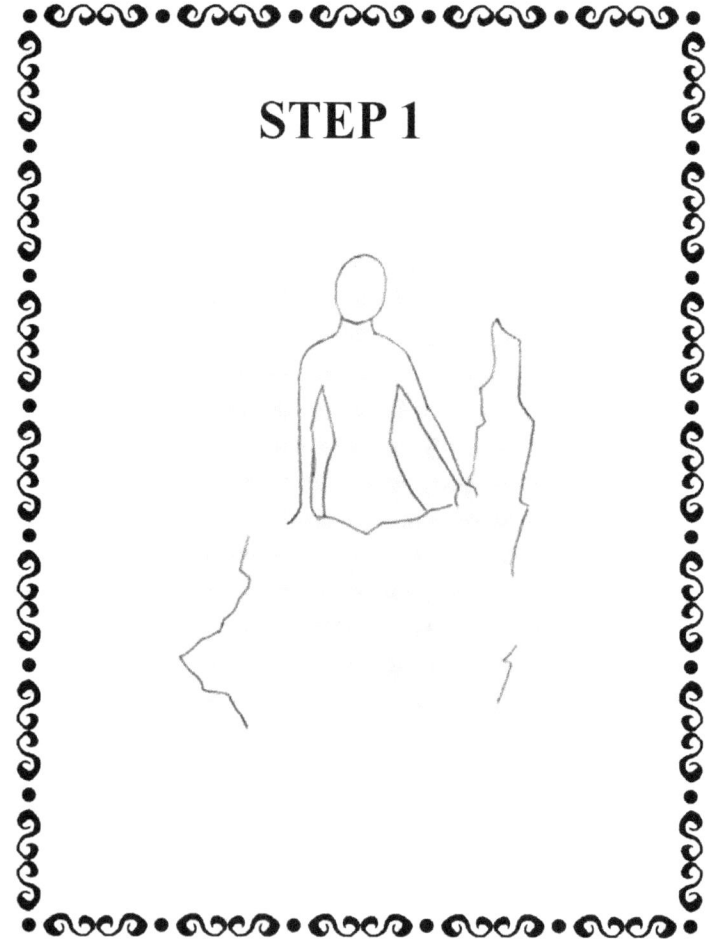

STEP 2

STEP 3

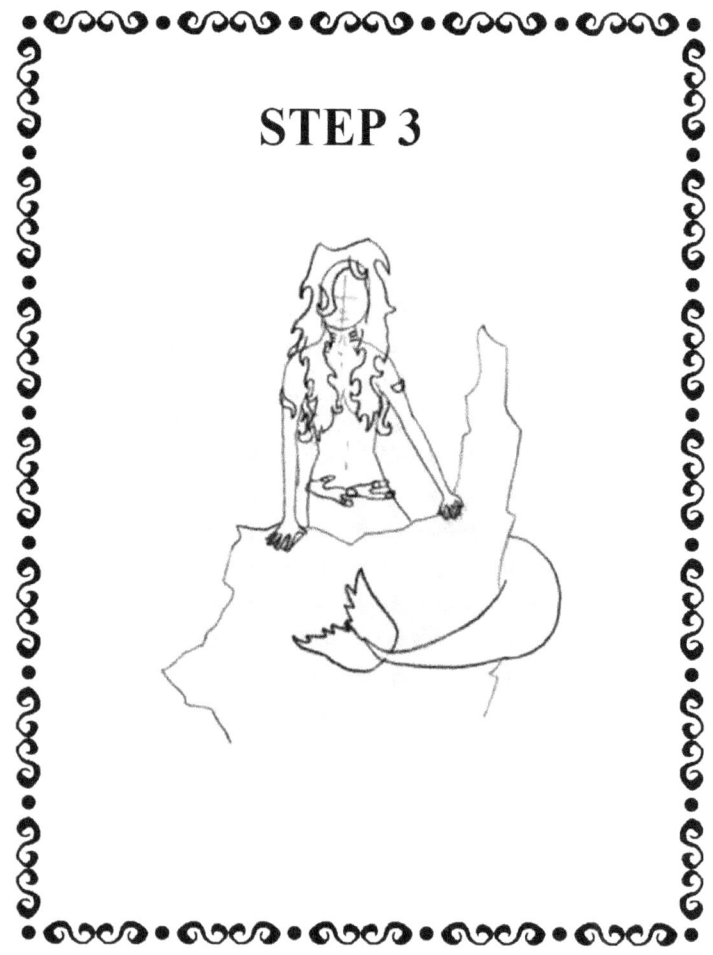

STEP 4

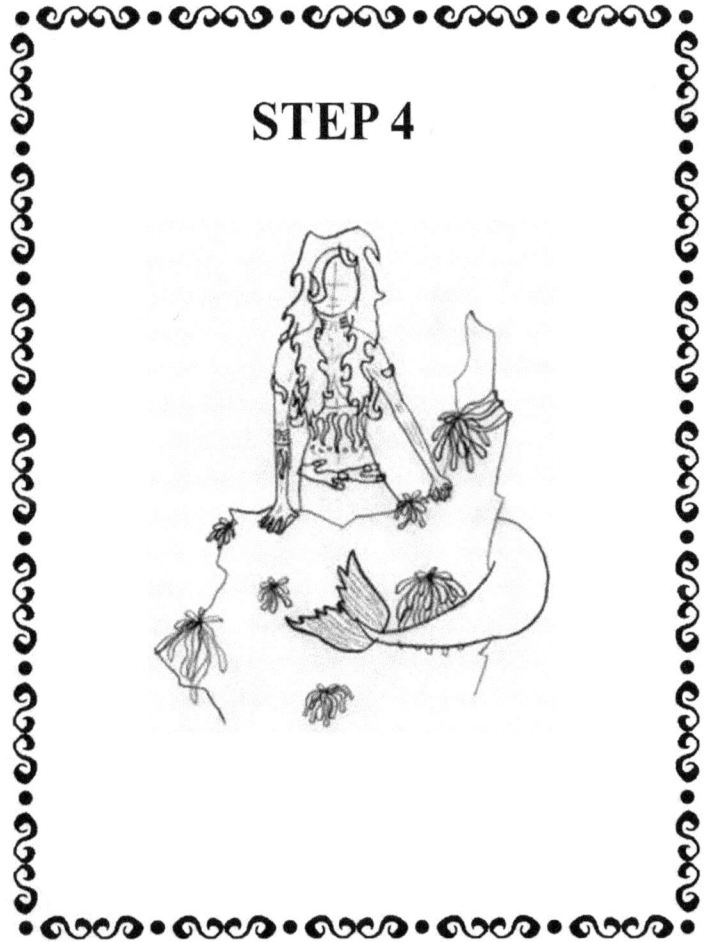

STEP 5

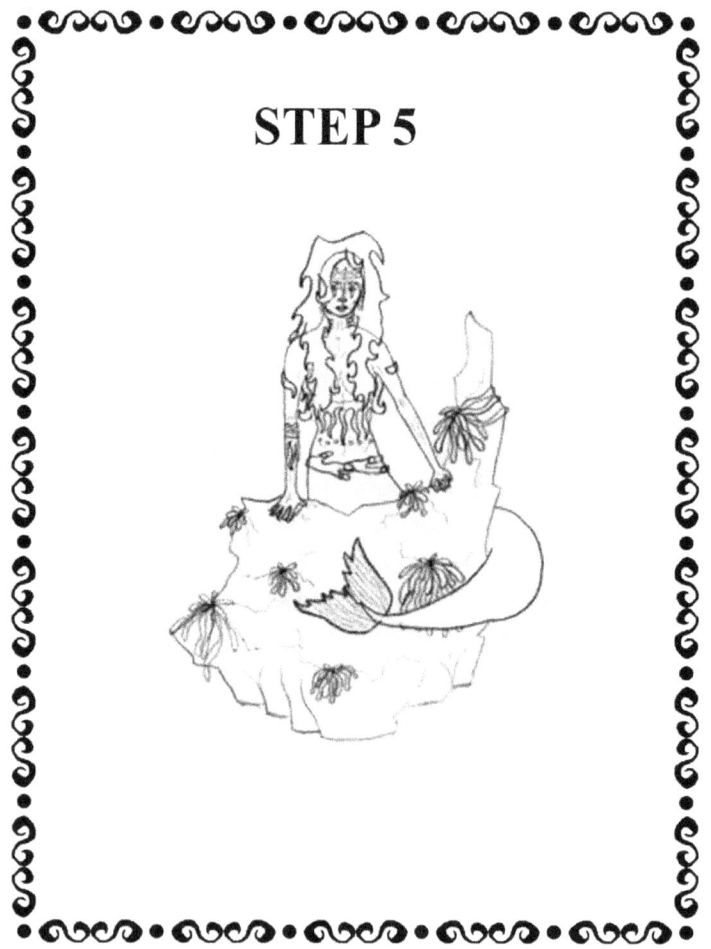

STEP 6

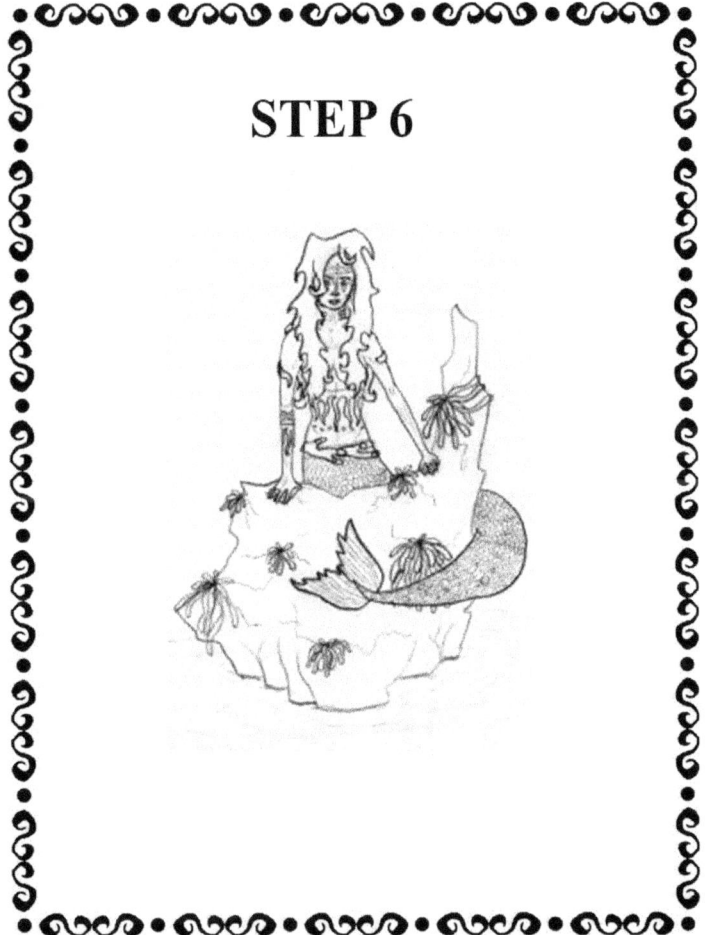

TAILED MERMAID

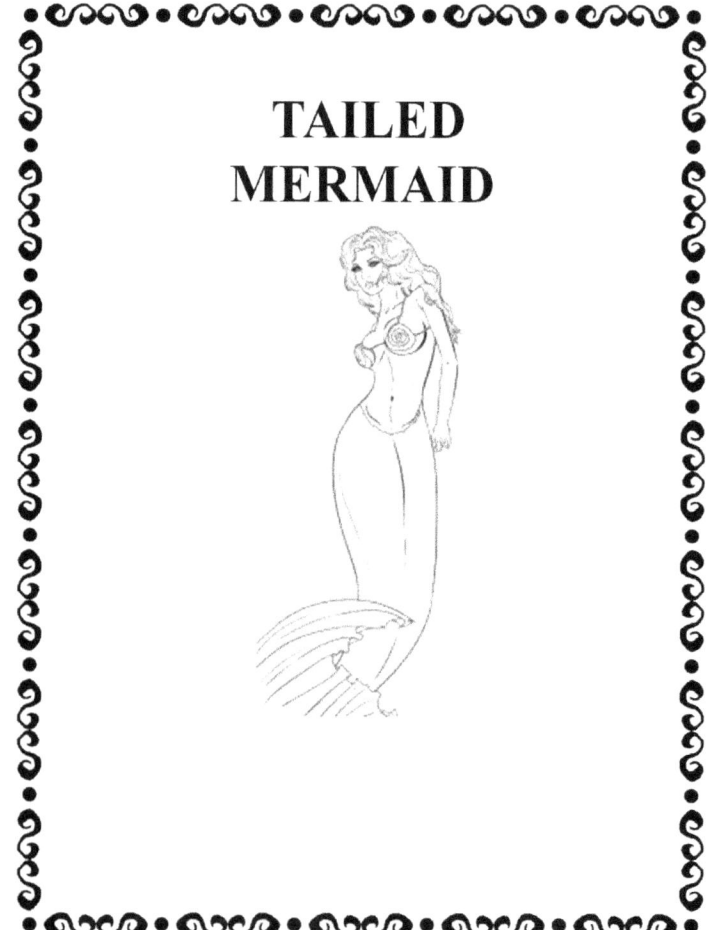

STEP 1

STEP 2

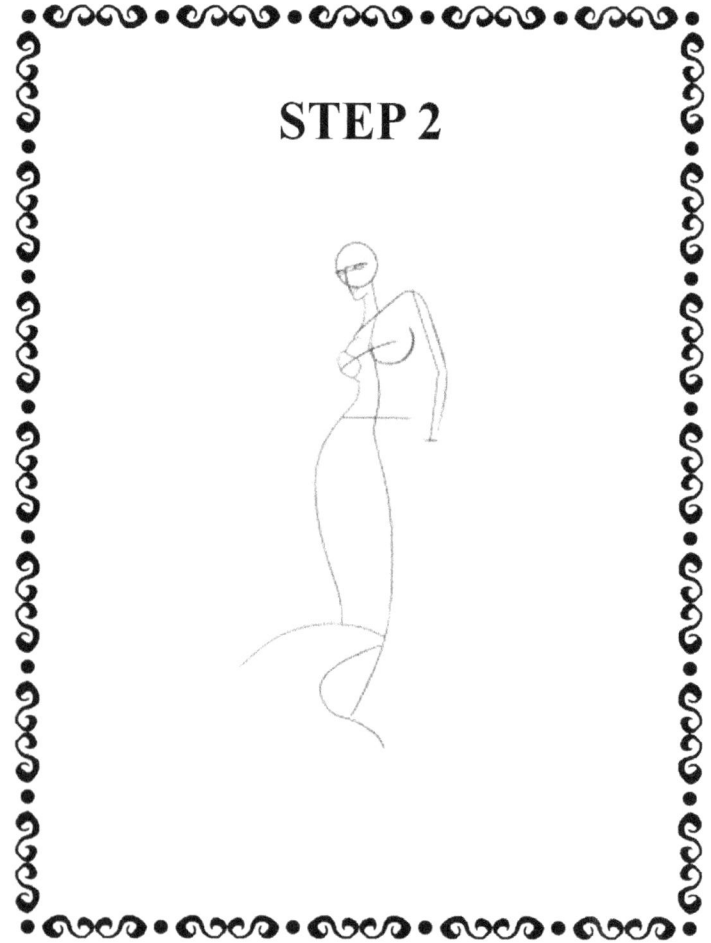

STEP 3

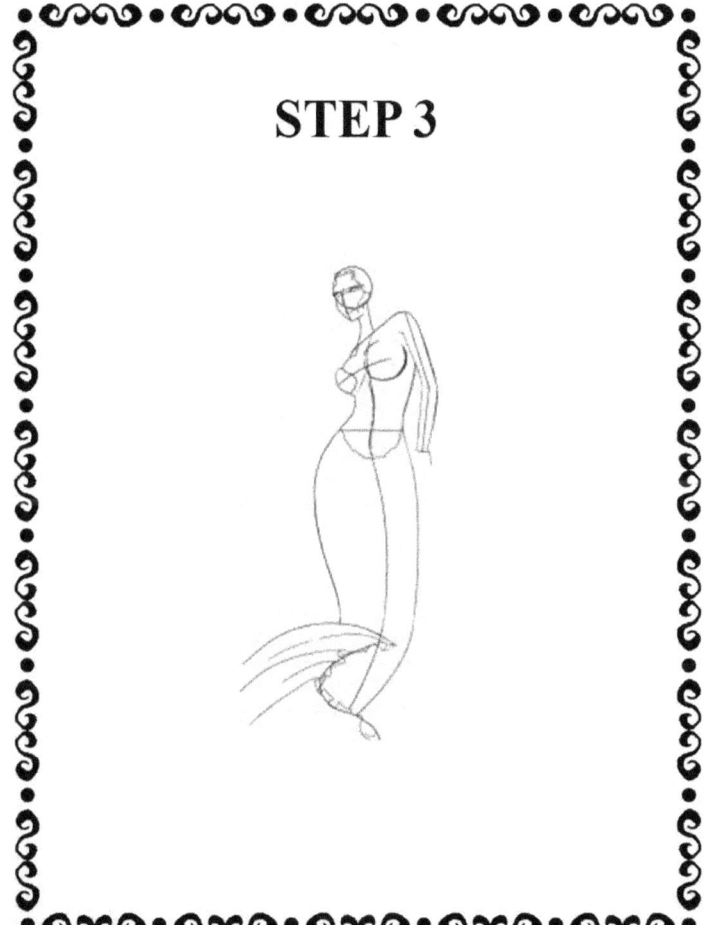

STEP 4

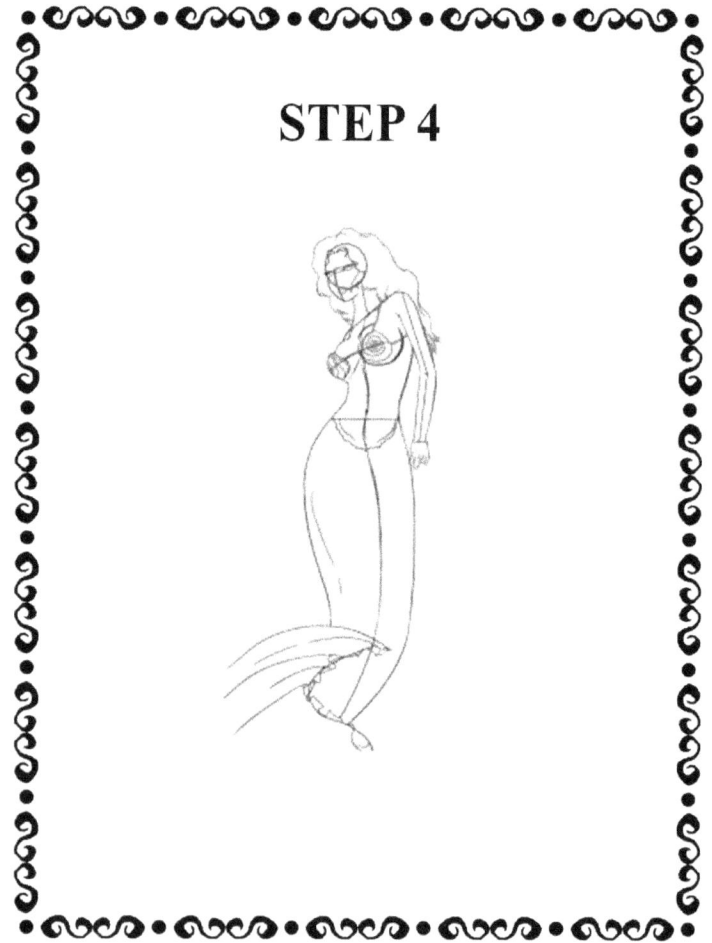

STEP 5